BLOOM



# Olympiad ACE

## A Comprehensive Practice Book

for School Olympiads & Talent Search Exams

# COMPUTER

## Class 3

by

Rashi Bansal

Olympiad ACE

BLOOM

Bloom Cap Edu Ventures Pvt. Ltd.



**Administrative & Production Office**

'Ramchhaya' 4577/15, Agarwal Road, Darya Ganj, New Delhi -110002

Tele: 011- 47630600, 43518550

**PRICE:** ₹125.00

Published by Arihant Publications (I) Ltd.

For further information about the books log on to www.bloomcap.org

Follow us on

# Preface

*"Future belongs to those Who prepares for it today"*

School Olympiads are National & International level competitions conducted by different Government, Non-Government & Educational Organisations with the purpose of making the children ready to face competitive exams.

The challenging Questions asked in Olympiads motivate them to learn more & more and bring out the best result with improved academic performance. The Awards & Scholarship offered by Olympiads motivate children to aspire & strive for doing better and emerge out to be the best.

## Science Olympiads

Being a Scientist or Engineer or Doctor has always been a dream of each school going child. A good command over Science is a must for any of these. Questions of Science Olympiads are structured to help students to develop scientific temperament & motivate them to understand the concepts of science. They also focuses on improving existing knowledge of a student by adding more information.

**'Bloom Science Olympiad Study Book Class 3'** is a perfect resource to Study & Practice for Olympiad Exams and other National & State Level Talent Search Exams & Other Competitions.

**Some Special Features of Bloom Science Olympiad Study Books are;**

- Chapterwise Exercises having different types of Objective Questions; Analytical, Applications, Remembering etc, at par with the Olympiad Level.
- Detailed Explanation for each question.
- Olympiad Pattern Practice Sets at the end.

This book is prepared by Expert Panel with the utmost care, still if you have any suggestions regarding its improvement then feel free to contact us at support@bloomcap.org. We will try to inculcate your suggestions in the further editions.

# Contents

# 01

# Fundamentals of Computer

1. The biggest advantage of a computer is that it is .................. in its operation.
   (a) slow in speed
   (b) required electricity
   (c) cost effective
   (d) automatic
2. Computers do not get tired like humans. What is this quality of computers called?
   (a) Reliability
   (b) Diligence
   (c) Versatility
   (d) Automation
3. .................. is the raw facts and figures.
   (a) Data (b) Information (c) Input (d) Byte
4. Which is a personal computer designed for regular use?
   (a) Desktop computer
   (b) Palmtop
   (c) Laptop
   (d) Minicomputer
5. ................ are the most powerful computers in the world.
   (a) Supercomputers
   (b) Mainframe computers
   (c) Mini computers
   (d) Microcomputers
6. A ............... has a battery inside it.
   (a) Laptop (b) Palmtop (c) Desktop (d) Both (a) and (b)
7. Which type of computers cannot be carried here and there?
   (a) Palmtop (b) Laptop (c) Desktop (d) Smartphone
8. Microcomputer is also known as
   (a) PC (Personal Computer)
   (b) Digital computer
   (c) Desktop computer
   (d) All of these

9. Which is not a function of Input Processing Output cycle function?
(a) It acts as the brain of the computer. (b) Every data or instruction is its input.
(c) Every action performed is a process. (d) The result of every action is input.

10. What will happen in a computer after input is taken and processing has been done?
(a) Output will be produced. (b) Input is taken again.
(c) More processing is done. (d) All of these

11. What does ALU stand for?
(a) Any Language Unit (b) Arithmetic Language Unit
(c) Arithmetic Logical Unit (d) None of these

12. What is a single binary digit also known as?
(a) Digit (b) Binary (c) Bit (d) None of these

13. Which was a mechanical computer designed by Charles Babbage?
(a) Punch Card (b) Analytical Engine
(c) Pasco (d) Difference Pascal

14. What was the processing speed of first generation computers?
(a) Milli-seconds (b) Micro-seconds (c) Nano-seconds (d) Pico-seconds

15. What is the capacity of a computer to store information called?
(a) Mouse (b) CPU (c) Monitor (d) Memory

16. The full form of the CPU is
(a) Computer Processing Unit (b) Computer Principle Unit
(c) Central Processing Unit (d) Control Processing Unit

17. A laptop computer works on
(a) battery (b) electricity (c) fuel (d) None of these

18. The computer helps in maintaining the accounts of ..................... in banks.
(a) patients (b) customers
(c) passengers (d) All of these

19. Computers help scientists in
(a) launching rockets (b) scientific research
(c) surfing in cyber cafes (d) Both (a) and (b)

20. ..................... is not a characteristic of a computer.
(a) Versatility (b) Accuracy (c) Diligence (d) IQ

21. Which of the following is the image of Abacus?

(a) 

(b) 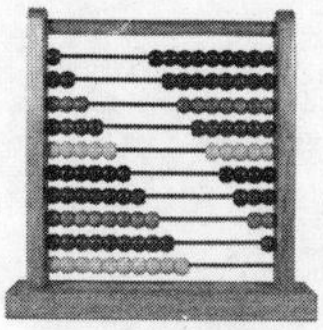

(c) 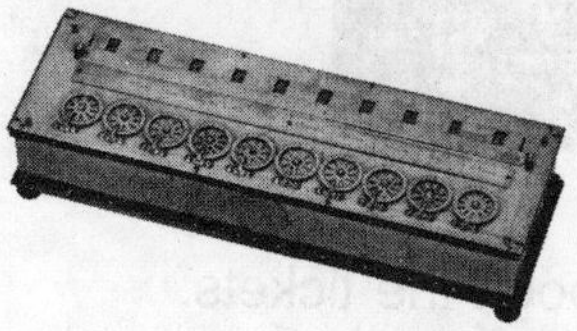

(d) 

**Direction** (Q 22-23) *On the basis of image given below, answer questions that follow.*

The image of a computer device is given below.

22. Which of the parts marked as P, Q, R and S is used to show the output?

(a) P
(b) Q
(c) R
(d) S

23. The part marked as P contains the processing unit, which comprises of

(a) Memory Unit
(b) Control Unit
(c) Arithmetic Logic Unit
(d) All of the above

24. Which of the following devices is not used to store data in the computer?

(a) 

(b) 

(c) 

(d) 

25. Identify the image where the computer is used to book the tickets.

(a) 

(b) 

(c) 

(d) 

26. Which of the following statements is/are true for computers?
(a) Computer is a machine or device that can perform arithmetical or logical operations automatically.
(b) Computers understand only binary language, which is written in the form of OS and IS.
(c) Computer is a programmable electronic device that stores, retrieves and processes the data.
(d) All of the above

27. Which of the following statements is false about computers?
(a) It is an electronic machine.
(b) It is cheaper than laptops.
(c) It stores, retrieves and processes data.
(d) It is powered by a rechargeable battery and that's why it needs to be charged regularly.

28. Select the incorrect match regarding uses of computers in various fields.
(a) Schools - Results
(b) Shops - Bills
(c) Offices - Eye testing
(d) Hospitals - Diagnosing Diseases

29. Match the following lists.

| List I | List II |
|---|---|
| A. To keep records of students | 1. In offices |
| B. To diagnose disease of patients | 2. In hotels |
| C. To prepare bills | 3. In hospitals |
| D. To prepare salary of employees | 4. At schools |

**Codes**

| | A | B | C | D | | A | B | C | D |
|---|---|---|---|---|---|---|---|---|---|
| (a) | 4 | 3 | 2 | 1 | (b) | 2 | 3 | 4 | 1 |
| (c) | 3 | 4 | 1 | 2 | (c) | 1 | 3 | 4 | 2 |

30. Match the following lists.

| List I | List II |
|---|---|
| A. Smallest unit of memory in computer | 1. Processing |
| B. Second stage of IPO | 2. Abacus |
| C. Binary system in a series of beads | 3. Intelligence Quotient |
| D. Missing in a computer | 4. Bit |

**Codes**

| | A | B | C | D | | A | B | C | D |
|---|---|---|---|---|---|---|---|---|---|
| (a) | 4 | 1 | 2 | 3 | (b) | 1 | 2 | 3 | 4 |
| (c) | 4 | 3 | 2 | 1 | (d) | 2 | 3 | 1 | 4 |

Darken your choice with HB Pencil

| | | | | | |
|---|---|---|---|---|---|
| 1. ⓐ ⓑ ⓒ ⓓ | 6. ⓐ ⓑ ⓒ ⓓ | 11. ⓐ ⓑ ⓒ ⓓ | 16. ⓐ ⓑ ⓒ ⓓ | 21. ⓐ ⓑ ⓒ ⓓ | 26. ⓐ ⓑ ⓒ ⓓ |
| 2. ⓐ ⓑ ⓒ ⓓ | 7. ⓐ ⓑ ⓒ ⓓ | 12. ⓐ ⓑ ⓒ ⓓ | 17. ⓐ ⓑ ⓒ ⓓ | 22. ⓐ ⓑ ⓒ ⓓ | 27. ⓐ ⓑ ⓒ ⓓ |
| 3. ⓐ ⓑ ⓒ ⓓ | 8. ⓐ ⓑ ⓒ ⓓ | 13. ⓐ ⓑ ⓒ ⓓ | 18. ⓐ ⓑ ⓒ ⓓ | 23. ⓐ ⓑ ⓒ ⓓ | 28. ⓐ ⓑ ⓒ ⓓ |
| 4. ⓐ ⓑ ⓒ ⓓ | 9. ⓐ ⓑ ⓒ ⓓ | 14. ⓐ ⓑ ⓒ ⓓ | 19. ⓐ ⓑ ⓒ ⓓ | 24. ⓐ ⓑ ⓒ ⓓ | 29. ⓐ ⓑ ⓒ ⓓ |
| 5. ⓐ ⓑ ⓒ ⓓ | 10. ⓐ ⓑ ⓒ ⓓ | 15. ⓐ ⓑ ⓒ ⓓ | 20. ⓐ ⓑ ⓒ ⓓ | 25. ⓐ ⓑ ⓒ ⓓ | 30. ⓐ ⓑ ⓒ ⓓ |

# 02

# Hardware and Software

1. Which one of the following is the main part of a computer?

(a) Mouse (b) CPU
(c) Motherboard (d) Monitor

2. The given image shows an example of

(a) Monochrome Monitor (b) CRT Monitor
(c) Keyboard (d) Touchscreen

3. Which of the following is an incorrect match?

(a) Pentium 5 - Scanner (b) CRT - Monitor
(c) QWERTY - Keyboard (d) Laser - Printer

4. Which computer peripheral device allows the computer to produce sound?

(a) Motherboard (b) SMPS
(c) Modem (d) Sound Card

5. Which storage device can store large data?

(a)  (b) 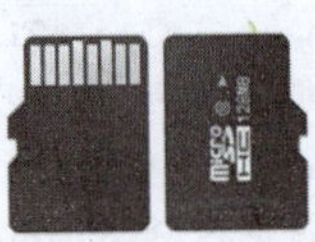 (c)  (d) 

6. Windows, Icons, Menus and Pointers are all part of
   (a) Graphical User Interface (b) Command Line Interface
   (c) Menu Interface (d) No User Interface

7. Which device is commonly used in shopping malls and large retail stores. What is this device called?

   (a) Organise keyboard (b) Concept keyboard
   (c) Active keyboard (d) Passive keyboard

8. Which of the following input devices is commonly found in Laptops?
   (a) Joystick (b) Touchpad
   (c) Printer (d) Light Pen

9. Choose the correct input and output devices.
   (a) Keyboard, Monitor (b) Printer, CPU
   (c) Monitor, Pendrive (d) All of these

10. What are input and output devices known as?
   (a) Interfaces (b) Interrupt
   (c) Computer peripherals (d) Input/Output Subsystem

11. Which of the following printers is suitable for continuous stationery paper?
   (a) Dot matrix printers (b) Daisy wheel printers
   (c) Inkjet printers (d) Laser printers

12. Which is an in-built storage device?
   (a) Compact Disc (b) Flash drive
   (c) Hard Disk (d) None of these

13. Which of the following keys is the longest key?
   (a) Backspace key (b) Spacebar key
   (c) Enter key (d) Control key

14. What keys can be found on a keyboard?
(a) Alphabet keys (b) Command keys
(c) Number keys (d) All of these

15. Identify the key that allows it to print.
(a) Ctrl + Print (b) Ctrl + P
(c) Alt + tab (d) Alt + P

16. Choose the software used for performing a certain type of work.
(a) Application software (b) System software
(c) Utility software (d) None of these

17. Monitor is also known as
(a) Memory Unit (b) Central Processing Unit
(c) Visual Display Unit (d) None of these

18. The ......... pen is an input device which is used to select and display objects on a computer screen.
(a) Ink (b) light
(c) magnetic (d) None of these

19. Scanner is a machine that
(a) print images (b) save images
(c) reproduces images onto a computer (d) draws pictures

20. The primary memory is located on the
(a) expansion board (b) motherboard
(c) storage device (d) output device

21 .........key takes the cursor to the next new line.
(a) Backspace (b) Spacebar
(c) Enter (d) Control

22. ......... is an example of Application software.
(a) Microsoft Word (b) Antivirus
(c) Microsoft Windows (d) Linux

23. Which among the following is a cursor control input device?

(a)  (b)  (c)  (d) 

**24.** Select the odd one out.

(a) 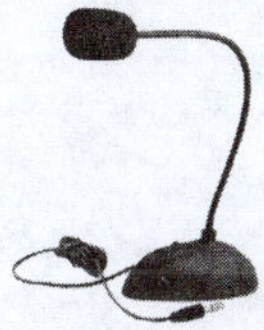 (b)  (c)  (d) 

**25.** Which of the following parts of the computer is used for reading or viewing a soft copy of a letter?

(a)  (b)  (c)  (d) 

**26.** Select the incorrect match.

| | List I | List II |
|---|---|---|
| (a) | Caps Lock | Used to type letters in capital |
| (b) | ⇧Shift | Used in combination with other keys for typing symbols |
| (c) | Backspace ← | Used to give space between letters or words |
| (d) | Esc | Used to cancel an operation |

**27.** Identify the correct pair of softwares on the basis of the given images.

(a) System software — Utility software
(b) System software — Application software
(c) Application software — Utility software
(d) None of the above

28. Match the following lists.

| List I | List II |
|---|---|
| A.  | 1. Uninterruptible Power Supply |
| B.  | 2. Barcode Reader |
| C.  | 3. Monitor |
| D.  | 4. Joystick |

**Codes**

| | A | B | C | D | | A | B | C | D |
|---|---|---|---|---|---|---|---|---|---|
| (a) | 3 | 1 | 2 | 4 | (b) | 2 | 3 | 4 | 1 |
| (c) | 2 | 1 | 3 | 4 | (d) | 1 | 2 | 3 | 4 |

29. Which of the following statements is incorrect?
(a) F1, F2,....F12 are number keys.
(b) Printouts are called hardcopies.
(c) Drag and drop by mouse is used to move the object from one position to another on the monitor.
(d) Spacebar is the longest key on the keyboard.

30. Choose the correct statement(s) for system software.
(a) Acts as an interface between the user and the computer hardware and manages transfer of data between them.
(b) Looks after the system security and performance.
(c) Allows smooth functioning of application software.
(d) All of the above

31. Match the following lists.

| | List I | | List II |
|---|---|---|---|
| A. | Stands for Read Only Memory | 1. | Linux |
| B. | It's a system software | 2. | Headphones |
| C. | Used to play games on computer | 3. | ROM |
| D. | Used to listen sound or music | 4. | Joystick |

**Codes**

| | A | B | C | D | | A | B | C | D |
|---|---|---|---|---|---|---|---|---|---|
| (a) | 3 | 4 | 1 | 2 | (b) | 3 | 1 | 4 | 2 |
| (c) | 2 | 3 | 4 | 1 | (d) | 4 | 1 | 2 | 3 |

32. Match the following lists.

| | List I | | List II |
|---|---|---|---|
| A. | Used to delete characters | 1. | Enter key |
| B. | Takes the cursor to the next new line | 2. | Caps Lock key |
| C. | Longest key | 3. | Backspace key |
| D. | Types the letter in capital | 4. | Spacebar key |

**Codes**

| | A | B | C | D | | A | B | C | D |
|---|---|---|---|---|---|---|---|---|---|
| (a) | 3 | 1 | 4 | 2 | (c) | 2 | 3 | 4 | 1 |
| (b) | 3 | 4 | 1 | 2 | (d) | 2 | 4 | 1 | 3 |

Darken your choice with HB Pencil

| | | | | | | | | | | | |
|---|---|---|---|---|---|---|---|---|---|---|---|
| 1. | ⓐ ⓑ ⓒ ⓓ | 7. | ⓐ ⓑ ⓒ ⓓ | 13. | ⓐ ⓑ ⓒ ⓓ | 19. | ⓐ ⓑ ⓒ ⓓ | 25. | ⓐ ⓑ ⓒ ⓓ | 31. | ⓐ ⓑ ⓒ ⓓ |
| 2. | ⓐ ⓑ ⓒ ⓓ | 8. | ⓐ ⓑ ⓒ ⓓ | 14. | ⓐ ⓑ ⓒ ⓓ | 20. | ⓐ ⓑ ⓒ ⓓ | 26. | ⓐ ⓑ ⓒ ⓓ | 32. | ⓐ ⓑ ⓒ ⓓ |
| 3. | ⓐ ⓑ ⓒ ⓓ | 9. | ⓐ ⓑ ⓒ ⓓ | 15. | ⓐ ⓑ ⓒ ⓓ | 21. | ⓐ ⓑ ⓒ ⓓ | 27. | ⓐ ⓑ ⓒ ⓓ | | |
| 4. | ⓐ ⓑ ⓒ ⓓ | 10. | ⓐ ⓑ ⓒ ⓓ | 16. | ⓐ ⓑ ⓒ ⓓ | 22. | ⓐ ⓑ ⓒ ⓓ | 28. | ⓐ ⓑ ⓒ ⓓ | | |
| 5. | ⓐ ⓑ ⓒ ⓓ | 11. | ⓐ ⓑ ⓒ ⓓ | 17. | ⓐ ⓑ ⓒ ⓓ | 23. | ⓐ ⓑ ⓒ ⓓ | 29. | ⓐ ⓑ ⓒ ⓓ | | |
| 6. | ⓐ ⓑ ⓒ ⓓ | 12. | ⓐ ⓑ ⓒ ⓓ | 18. | ⓐ ⓑ ⓒ ⓓ | 24. | ⓐ ⓑ ⓒ ⓓ | 30. | ⓐ ⓑ ⓒ ⓓ | | |

# 03

# Understanding Windows

1. Which of the following terms is used for individual items on a computer, such as a word document, an image, etc.?
(a) File (b) Folder (c) Directory (d) Library

2. Which of the following is not a part of the Windows Accessories folder?
(a) MS Paint (b) Notepad
(c) Disk Cleanup (d) Character Map

3. Identify the icon and choose the application to which it belongs.

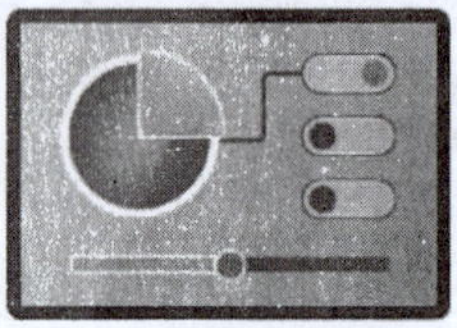

(a) Microsoft Edge (b) Control Panel (c) PC (d) Recycle Bin

4. In any window, the maximise button, the minimise button and the close button appear on
(a) Tool bar (b) Title bar (c) Menu bar (d) Status bar

5. To 'Maximise' a window means
(a) drag it on the Recycle Bin (b) put only like files inside
(c) expand it to fit the desktop (d) fill it to capacity

6. To deselect an icon, we should click
(a) on the icon (b) away from the icon
(c) inside the icon (d) None of these

7. Which function key is used for opening help?
(a) F1 (b) F2 (c) F3 (d) F4

8. What does C in CUI stands for
(a) Common (b) Casual (c) Character (d) None of these

9. To set your desktop's background and themes, you should
(a) right click on the desktop and click Personalise.
(b) type Personalisation in the Search Box of the Start Menu and press Enter Key.
(c) Both (a) and (b)
(d) None of the above

10. Which of the following steps will add a clock on your desktop?

(a) Right click the desktop → Gadgets (b) Right click the desktop → Clock
(c) Right click the desktop → Settings (d) All of these

11. The small labelled pictures present on the desktop are called
(a) mouse (b) background (c) icons (d) images

12. ......... developed the Windows Operating System.
(a) Cray Industries (b) Microsoft Corporation
(c) ISRO (d) Apple Inc.

13. Who is the founder of Microsoft?
(a) Bill Gates (b) Charles Babbage
(c) Donald Trump (d) None of these

14. The Start menu in Windows 7 is divided into ............ parts.
(a) one (b) two (c) three (d) four

15. What is the first screen that appears after loading the operating system called?
(a) Desktop (b) First screen (c) Monitor (d) Taskbar

16. GUI stands for
(a) Graphical User Interface (b) Grapevine User Interface
(c) Graphical User Interleave (d) None of these

17. Identify the following.
I. It is the file manager that allows users to manage files and folders.
II. It can be used to navigate the hard drive and display the contents of the folders.
(a) Windows Manager (b) File Explorer
(c) File Handler (d) Control Panel

18. What is an Address Bar?
    (a) A software that controls the basic operations of your computer.
    (b) A folder that stores the files you want to delete and allows you to restore them if needed.
    (c) A program used to show thumbnails.
    (d) A text box that identifies the path for the currently opened folder.

19. Which of the following Windows does not have a Start button?
    (a) Windows 7 (b) Windows 8
    (c) Windows 10 (d) None of these

20. Which operating system is this symbol of ?

    (a) Mac OS X (b) Linux (c) Windows (d) Android

21. Windows 7 is designed to
    (a) sleep and resume faster (b) use up less memory
    (c) recognize USB devices faster (d) All of these

22. The image displayed here is the image of

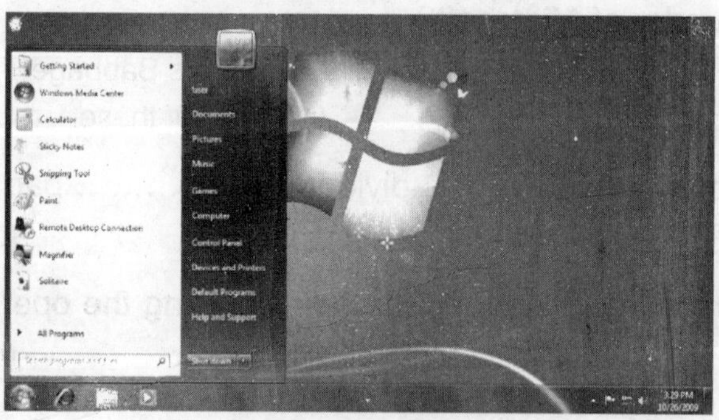


    (a) Windows Explorer (b) Desktop
    (c) Control Panel (d) Start Menu

23. Identify the image given below and choose the correct option.

    (a) Desktop (b) Start Tab
    (c) Taskbar (d) Status Bar

24. Identify the network icon.

(a)  (b)  (c)  (d) 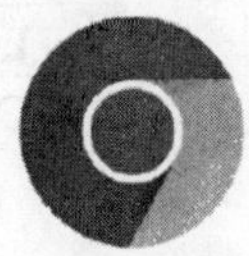

25. What is the keyboard shortcut for power use mode in Windows 10?

(a) Windows key + S (b) Windows key + X
(c) Windows key + U (d) Windows key + V

26. Identify the image given below and choose the correct option.

(a) Taskbar (b) Start Tab
(c) Notification Area (d) Quick Launcher

27. Identify the icon given below.

(a) Control Panel (b) My Computer
(c) Internet Explorer (d) Microsoft Windows

28. The left-most part of Taskbar contains the .............. and .............. to the right-most area.

(a) start button, notification area (b) search tool, quick launcher
(c) notification area, wallpaper (d) None of these

29. What is the icon for an empty folder in Windows 10 desktop by default?

(a) An empty wallet (b) An empty file
(c) An empty trash bin paper folder (d) An empty trash bin

30. Which of the following is not a part of Windows 10 desktop by default?

(a) Icons (b) Wallpaper
(c) Taskbar (d) Shortcuts

31. Which keyboard shortcut is used to close the active documents in Windows 10?

(a) Ctrl+A (b) Ctrl+F4 (c) Ctrl+C (d) Ctrl+V

32. Match the following lists.

| List I | List II |
|---|---|
| A. Clock Gadget | 1. 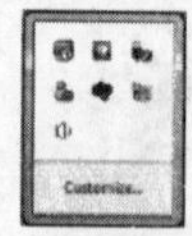 |
| B. System Tray | 2.  |
| C. Start Button | 3.  |
| D. Recycle Bin | 4.  |

**Codes**

| | A | B | C | D | | A | B | C | D |
|---|---|---|---|---|---|---|---|---|---|
| (a) | 4 | 2 | 3 | 1 | (b) | 1 | 4 | 2 | 3 |
| (c) | 3 | 1 | 4 | 2 | (d) | 2 | 3 | 1 | 4 |

33. Match the following lists.

| List I | List II |
|---|---|
| A. System Tray | 1. Background picture on the desktop. |
| B. Wallpaper | 2. Start button is a part of it on the desktop. |
| C. Taskbar | 3. Temporarily stores the deleted items from computer. |
| D. Recycle Bin | 4. Shows date, time and notifications on desktop. |

**Codes**

| | A | B | C | D | | A | B | C | D |
|---|---|---|---|---|---|---|---|---|---|
| (a) | 4 | 1 | 2 | 3 | (b) | 3 | 2 | 1 | 4 |
| (c) | 4 | 2 | 1 | 3 | (d) | 2 | 3 | 1 | 4 |

Darken your choice with HB Pencil

| | | | | | |
|---|---|---|---|---|---|
| 1. ⓐ ⓑ ⓒ ⓓ | 7. ⓐ ⓑ ⓒ ⓓ | 13. ⓐ ⓑ ⓒ ⓓ | 19. ⓐ ⓑ ⓒ ⓓ | 25. ⓐ ⓑ ⓒ ⓓ | 31. ⓐ ⓑ ⓒ ⓓ |
| 2. ⓐ ⓑ ⓒ ⓓ | 8. ⓐ ⓑ ⓒ ⓓ | 14. ⓐ ⓑ ⓒ ⓓ | 20. ⓐ ⓑ ⓒ ⓓ | 26. ⓐ ⓑ ⓒ ⓓ | 32. ⓐ ⓑ ⓒ ⓓ |
| 3. ⓐ ⓑ ⓒ ⓓ | 9. ⓐ ⓑ ⓒ ⓓ | 15. ⓐ ⓑ ⓒ ⓓ | 21. ⓐ ⓑ ⓒ ⓓ | 27. ⓐ ⓑ ⓒ ⓓ | 33. ⓐ ⓑ ⓒ ⓓ |
| 4. ⓐ ⓑ ⓒ ⓓ | 10. ⓐ ⓑ ⓒ ⓓ | 16. ⓐ ⓑ ⓒ ⓓ | 22. ⓐ ⓑ ⓒ ⓓ | 28. ⓐ ⓑ ⓒ ⓓ | |
| 5. ⓐ ⓑ ⓒ ⓓ | 11. ⓐ ⓑ ⓒ ⓓ | 17. ⓐ ⓑ ⓒ ⓓ | 23. ⓐ ⓑ ⓒ ⓓ | 29. ⓐ ⓑ ⓒ ⓓ | |
| 6. ⓐ ⓑ ⓒ ⓓ | 12. ⓐ ⓑ ⓒ ⓓ | 18. ⓐ ⓑ ⓒ ⓓ | 24. ⓐ ⓑ ⓒ ⓓ | 30. ⓐ ⓑ ⓒ ⓓ | |

04

# MS Paint 2016

1. Which bar holds the buttons to do common tasks?
(a) Title bar (b) Quick access toolbar
(c) Toolbar (d) None of these

2. Which shortcut is used for cutting the image?
(a) Ctrl + V (b) Ctrl + X (c) Ctrl + C (d) Ctrl + Z

3. Which handle allows the image to be resized diagonally?
(a) Sizing handle (b) Corner handle (c) Oblique handle (d) All of the abovc

4. Which of the following options is used to view the drawing as it will look when printed?
(a) Print preview (b) Pago setup (c) Print selected (d) Page layout

5. The height and width of the drawing area can be changed by using
(a) Image group → Resize → Rotate 90°
(b) Image group → Resize → Flip Vertical
(c) Paint button → Properties → Set the value of Width and Height
(d) All of the above

6. What is the shortcut key to print any document in MS Paint?
(a) Ctrl + S (b) Ctrl + J (c) Alt + P (d) Ctrl + P

7. Which of the following can create an effect that can be used in making an illusion of 3D perspective?
(a) Skew (b) Flip (c) Rotate (d) Stretch

8. The paint window is divided into .............. parts.
(a) one (b) two (c) three (d) four

9. Which tool is used for drawing a straight line?
(a) Line Tool (b) Straight Tool (c) Scale Tool (d) Pencil

10. What is the name of the tool used to zoom the pictures?
(a) Text Tool (b) Magnifier Tool (c) Pick Tool (d) Line Tool

11. Which is the shortcut key to save a drawing?
(a) Ctrl + O (b) Ctrl + S (c) Ctrl + V (d) None of these

12. To open MS Paint, we Select Start → X → Accessories → Paint. What is X?
(a) Tool Box (b) List Box (c) All Programs (d) None of these

13. There is a collection of readymade graphic images on the computer. What is this image called?
(a) Wonderful Art (b) Art and Craft (c) Clip Art (d) None of these

14. Which is not a readymade shape?
(a)  (b) 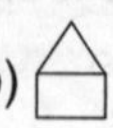 (c)  (d) 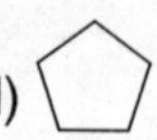

15. In MS Paint, .............. is used for spraying the color.
(a) pencil (b) airbrush (c) dropper (d) brush

16. The Paint Brush opens and saves files with the .............. extension.
(a) .doc (b) .ppt (c) .txt (d) .bmp

17. .............. is a tool used to draw thin, free form lines or curves.
(a) Pencil (b) Pen (c) Brush (d) Line

18. .............. is the shortcut key or quick key to undo the last change you made.
(a) Ctrl+Z (b) Ctrl+U
(c) Ctrl+S (d) Ctrl+D

19. .............. and .............. are two selection tools in MS Paint.
(a) Rectangular, Circular (b) Free form, Circular
(c) Free form, Rectangular (d) None of these

20. Which operation would change the image X to image Y?

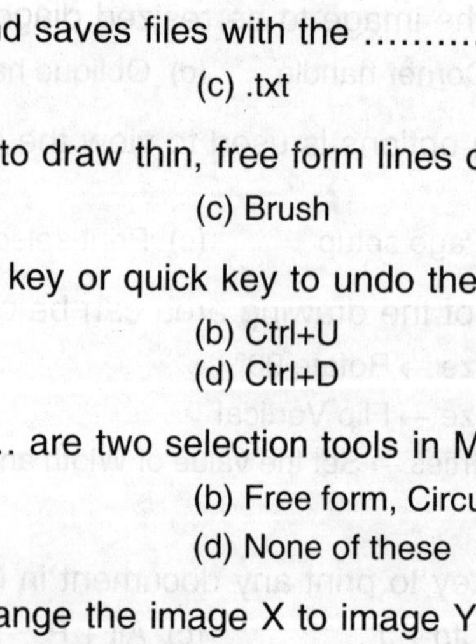

(a) Flip Vertical (b) Skew (c) Rotate 180 (d) Flip Horizontal

21. What is the area pointed by X in the image called?

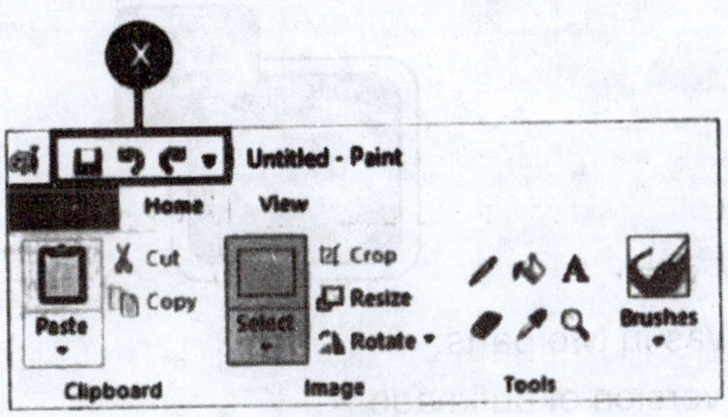


(a) Ribbon
(b) Quick Access
(c) Menu Bar
(d) Title Bar

22. Which of the following is not a correct method to clear your documents of all work?

(a) Select the area with press  key.


(b) Select the area with press 'click Cut'.

(c) Select the area with press click .

(d) Soloct the area with select .

23. How to duplicate a picture?

(a) Draw again
(b) Copy, Paste
(c) Select, Copy, Paste
(d) Cut

24. Which icon is the Microsoft Paint?

(a)  (b)  (c)  (d) 

25. What is the function of the given icon?

(a) It divides the canvas in two parts.
(b) It shows a larger version of an image.
(c) It shows the frame on the picture.
(d) It is used for viewing a smaller version of a drawing in a separate window, when you have enabled the zoom-in feature.

26. Select the odd one out regarding shapes found in MS Paint.

(a) 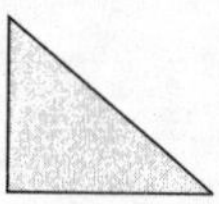 (b) 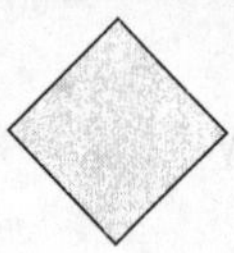 (c)  (d) 

27. Match the following lists.

| List I | List II |
|---|---|
| A.  | 1. To draw a perfect square |
| B.  | 2. For free hand drawing |
| C.  | 3. To add text to drawing |
| D.  | 4. To fill an area with the current color |

**Codes**

| | A | B | C | D | | A | B | C | D |
|---|---|---|---|---|---|---|---|---|---|
| (a) | 1 | 3 | 2 | 4 | (b) | 4 | 1 | 3 | 2 |
| (c) | 1 | 4 | 3 | 2 | (d) | 4 | 1 | 2 | 3 |

28. Choose the correct statement.
(a) MS Paint allows us to draw and color drawings.
(b) MS Paint allows us to watch a video.
(c) MS Paint allows us to play games.
(d) MS Paint allows us to watch a movie.

29. Match the following lists.

| List I | List II |
|---|---|
| A. Color Picker Tool | 1. Used for zooming in and out of drawing area. |
| B. Magnifier Tool | 2. Used for copying color from one figure to another. |
| C. Rectangular Selection | 3. Shapes used to draw traffic light. |
| D. Circle and Rectangle | 4. Used to select a rectangular area. |

**Codes**

| | A | B | C | D | | A | B | C | D |
|---|---|---|---|---|---|---|---|---|---|
| (a) | 4 | 2 | 1 | 3 | (b) | 3 | 4 | 2 | 1 |
| (c) | 1 | 3 | 4 | 2 | (d) | 2 | 1 | 4 | 3 |

Darken your choice with HB Pencil

| | | | | | | | | | | | |
|---|---|---|---|---|---|---|---|---|---|---|---|
| **1.** | ⓐ ⓑ ⓒ ⓓ | **6.** | ⓐ ⓑ ⓒ ⓓ | **11.** | ⓐ ⓑ ⓒ ⓓ | **16.** | ⓐ ⓑ ⓒ ⓓ | **21.** | ⓐ ⓑ ⓒ ⓓ | **26.** | ⓐ ⓑ ⓒ ⓓ |
| **2.** | ⓐ ⓑ ⓒ ⓓ | **7.** | ⓐ ⓑ ⓒ ⓓ | **12.** | ⓐ ⓑ ⓒ ⓓ | **17.** | ⓐ ⓑ ⓒ ⓓ | **22.** | ⓐ ⓑ ⓒ ⓓ | **27.** | ⓐ ⓑ ⓒ ⓓ |
| **3.** | ⓐ ⓑ ⓒ ⓓ | **8.** | ⓐ ⓑ ⓒ ⓓ | **13.** | ⓐ ⓑ ⓒ ⓓ | **18.** | ⓐ ⓑ ⓒ ⓓ | **23.** | ⓐ ⓑ ⓒ ⓓ | **28.** | ⓐ ⓑ ⓒ ⓓ |
| **4.** | ⓐ ⓑ ⓒ ⓓ | **9.** | ⓐ ⓑ ⓒ ⓓ | **14.** | ⓐ ⓑ ⓒ ⓓ | **19.** | ⓐ ⓑ ⓒ ⓓ | **24.** | ⓐ ⓑ ⓒ ⓓ | **29.** | ⓐ ⓑ ⓒ ⓓ |
| **5.** | ⓐ ⓑ ⓒ ⓓ | **10.** | ⓐ ⓑ ⓒ ⓓ | **15.** | ⓐ ⓑ ⓒ ⓓ | **20.** | ⓐ ⓑ ⓒ ⓓ | **25.** | ⓐ ⓑ ⓒ ⓓ | | |

# 05

# Introduction to MS Word 2016

1. Which of the following is a Microsoft Word software?
   (a) Paint
   (b) Word processing
   (c) MS DOS
   (d) None of these
2. Which is not used in MS Word?
   (a) Italic
   (b) Magic Tool
   (c) Font
   (d) Bold
3. Which keyboard shortcut is used to open a new file?
   (a) Ctrl+N
   (b) Ctrl+Z
   (c) Ctrl+U
   (d) Ctrl+S
4. How many ways are there to save a document?
   (a) Four
   (b) Three
   (c) Two
   (d) One
5. Which of the following is not a font style?
   (a) Italics
   (b) Bold
   (c) Superscript
   (d) Font size
6. ……… is the default font of Word 2016.
   (a) Times New Roman
   (b) Georgia
   (c) Calibri
   (d) Arial
7. ……… means changing the appearance of a document.
   (a) Editing
   (b) Formatting
   (c) Changing
   (d) None of these

8. Which option emphasises the text by slanting it to the right?
(a) Bold (b) Italic (c) Underline (d) None of these

9. By default, text is aligned to the
(a) Left (b) Right (c) Center (d) Justify

10. Which of the following is/are word processing software?
(a) Word Perfect (b) Word Pad (c) MS Word (d) All of these

11. The ......... works with the standard Copy and Paste commands.
(a) View Tab (b) Paragraph Dialog Box
(c) Office Clipboard (d) All of these

12. Which is an example of Page Orientation?
(a) Landscape (b) Subscript (c) Superscript (d) Alignment

13. The bold button is used to display the text in a ......... shade than the rest of the text.
(a) lighter (b) darker (c) bigger (d) smaller

14. Which case on application turns 'AmAzINg' to 'aMaZinG'?
(a) Toggle key (b) Uppercase (c) Lowercase (d) Sentence case

15. What is the blank space outside the printing area on a page called?
(a) Clipart (b) Margins (c) Header (d) Footer

16. The size of the area in which you want to type the text or align the text can be set by
(a) Scroll Bar (b) Ruler (c) Status Bar (d) None of these

17. Which of the following options is used to repeat the last work done in a document?
(a) Redo (b) Undo (c) Paste (d) Copy

18. By clicking inside the font size box, you can
(a) only decrease the font size
(b) only increase the font size
(c) set the font size to anything you want
(d) All of the above

19. For closing the file in MS Word 2016, ......... shortcut is used.
(a) Alt+F4 (b) Shift+F6 (c) Alt+Shift (d) Ctrl+F4

20. ......... is used to save a file in MS Word.
(a) Ctrl+S (b) Ctrl+O (c) Ctrl+V (d) None of these

21. To close MS Word, click the file button and then
(a) exit (b) save (c) open (d) None of these

22. A file can be saved by clicking on the ............... button on the Quick Access Toolbar.
(a) close (b) print (c) save (d) None of these

23. Given here is an image of options available in the Clipboard group of Home tab. Which of the following tasks is not possible with the help of these options?

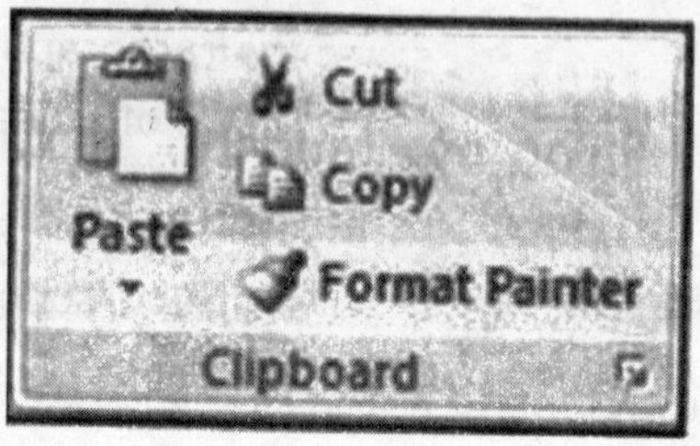


(a) Removing a line of text (b) Copying a line of text
(c) Repeating the last operation (d) Pasting a copied part

24. Which of the following is found in the File tab?

(a) 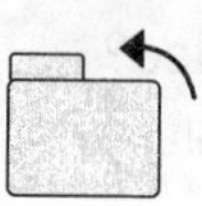 (b)  (c) 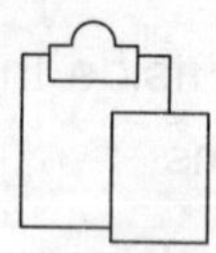 (d) 

25. Given below is the Title bar of an MS Word document. It displays the ............... of the active document.

(a) area (b) color (c) height (d) name

26. Which of the following keys, when pressed, will allow you to jump directly to the beginning of a line if you are in the middle of the line?

(a) 

(b) 

(c) 

(d) 

27. Which of the following statements is incorrect?
(a) Copying of text removes the original text from its original position.
(b) There can be two scrollbars to a word document.
(c) The Bold effect makes the text go thicker.
(d) The Ctrl+C shortcut copies the highlighted text.

**28.** Match the following lists.

| List I | List II |
|---|---|
| A. Ctrl+X | 1. To paste the text |
| B. Ctrl+S | 2. To cut the selected text |
| C. Ctrl+V | 3. To copy the selected text |
| D. Ctrl+C | 4. To save a document |

**Codes**

| | A | B | C | D | | A | B | C | D |
|---|---|---|---|---|---|---|---|---|---|
| (a) | 3 | 4 | 2 | 1 | (b) | 2 | 4 | 1 | 3 |
| (c) | 1 | 2 | 3 | 4 | (d) | 4 | 3 | 1 | 2 |

**29.** Match the following lists.

| List I | List II |
|---|---|
| A. Font group | 1. You can increase or decrease font size |
| B. Center Alignment | 2. Effects like Bold, Italic and Underline |
| C. Commands in Font group | 3. Ctrl+E is a keyboard shortcut |
| D. To highlight text | 4. Format painter is not its part |

**Codes**

| | A | B | C | D | | A | B | C | D |
|---|---|---|---|---|---|---|---|---|---|
| (a) | 3 | 4 | 2 | 1 | (b) | 2 | 1 | 3 | 4 |
| (c) | 1 | 2 | 4 | 3 | (d) | 4 | 3 | 1 | 2 |

Darken your choice with HB Pencil

| | | | | | | | | | | | |
|---|---|---|---|---|---|---|---|---|---|---|---|
| **1.** | ⓐ ⓑ ⓒ ⓓ | **6.** | ⓐ ⓑ ⓒ ⓓ | **11.** | ⓐ ⓑ ⓒ ⓓ | **16.** | ⓐ ⓑ ⓒ ⓓ | **21.** | ⓐ ⓑ ⓒ ⓓ | **26.** | ⓐ ⓑ ⓒ ⓓ |
| **2.** | ⓐ ⓑ ⓒ ⓓ | **7.** | ⓐ ⓑ ⓒ ⓓ | **12.** | ⓐ ⓑ ⓒ ⓓ | **17.** | ⓐ ⓑ ⓒ ⓓ | **22.** | ⓐ ⓑ ⓒ ⓓ | **27.** | ⓐ ⓑ ⓒ ⓓ |
| **3.** | ⓐ ⓑ ⓒ ⓓ | **8.** | ⓐ ⓑ ⓒ ⓓ | **13.** | ⓐ ⓑ ⓒ ⓓ | **18.** | ⓐ ⓑ ⓒ ⓓ | **23.** | ⓐ ⓑ ⓒ ⓓ | **28.** | ⓐ ⓑ ⓒ ⓓ |
| **4.** | ⓐ ⓑ ⓒ ⓓ | **9.** | ⓐ ⓑ ⓒ ⓓ | **14.** | ⓐ ⓑ ⓒ ⓓ | **19.** | ⓐ ⓑ ⓒ ⓓ | **24.** | ⓐ ⓑ ⓒ ⓓ | **29.** | ⓐ ⓑ ⓒ ⓓ |
| **5.** | ⓐ ⓑ ⓒ ⓓ | **10.** | ⓐ ⓑ ⓒ ⓓ | **15.** | ⓐ ⓑ ⓒ ⓓ | **20.** | ⓐ ⓑ ⓒ ⓓ | **25.** | ⓐ ⓑ ⓒ ⓓ | | |

06

# Introduction to Internet

1. What is Internet?
   (a) A network of networks
   (b) A single network
   (c) Multiple networks
   (d) None of these
2. Website is a collection of
   (a) HTML documents
   (b) audio video files
   (c) graphic files
   (d) All of these
3. WWW stands for
   (a) World Wide Web
   (b) Wide World Web
   (c) Web World Web
   (d) None of these
4. Who founded WWW?
   (a) Tim Berners Lee
   (b) Bill Gates
   (c) Charles Babbage
   (d) Dennis Ritchie
5. Which of the following is the first page of a website?
   (a) First page
   (b) New page
   (c) Home page
   (d) Title page
6. Which of the following is a disadvantage of the Internet?
   (a) Searching and reading books
   (b) Virus threat
   (c) Buying and selling products
   (d) Filling an online form
7. What is online?
   (a) When you are connected to the internet through an ISP or a network.
   (b) When you yourself go on the internet.
   (c) When you are connected to a telephone.
   (d) None of the above

8. Objective of the web server is/are to ............... to the users.
(a) store web pages
(b) process web pages
(c) deliver web pages
(d) All of these

9. 'http//www.google.com' is an example of
(a) website
(b) webpage
(c) search engine
(d) Uniform Resource Locator

10. In LAN, 'A' stands for
(a) Access
(b) Attribute
(c) Area
(d) Administrator

11. What kind of a network can span to a kilometer?
(a) LAN
(b) CAN
(c) WAN
(d) MAN

12. What is the other name of Internet?
(a) Connect
(b) Net
(c) Cyber
(d) Social

13. The first widely popular browser was
(a) Mosaic
(b) ARPANET
(c) Internet Explorer
(d) Google

14. What does A stands in ARPANET?
(a) Automatic
(b) Assured
(c) Arranged
(d) Advanced

15. ........................... is not required to connect to the internet.
(a) A computer system
(b) A modem
(c) A website
(d) A web browser

16. Identify the image and name the technology which is used to access the internet.

(a) Wi-Fi (Wireless Fidelity)
(b) Mobile data
(c) Wired connection
(d) Connection through telephone line

17. In E-Mail, E stands for
(a) electric
(b) electronic
(c) engine
(d) None of these

18. Which of the following is an ISP?

(a) G (b) airtel (c) SONY (d) YAHOO!

19. ............... is a collection of web pages.

(a) Website (b) URL
(c) Web browser (d) Home page

20. The term internet was derived from the word

(a) interacted networks
(b) interconnected networks
(c) international networks
(d) incorporated networks

21. You cannot connect the internet through

(a)  (b)  (c)  (d) 

22. Unscramble the word given here and select the icon it represents in Windows 7.
TRTIENE POLEREXR

(a) 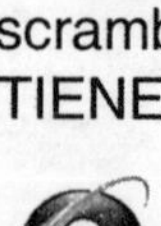 (b)  (c)  (d) 

23. Which of the following images cannot be connected to the internet?

(a)  (b)  (c)  (d) 

24. Which of the following is not a search engine?

(a) yahoo! (b) Google (c) Bing (d) 

25. Identify the image and choose the correct statement(s) about it.

(a) It is known as Modem or Modulator Demodulator.
(b) It can be fitted into the computer (internal modem) or attached from outside (external modem).
(c) It is provided to the user by Internet Service Providers (ISP).
(d) All of the above

26. Choose the correct option(s).
(a) Internet connection is provided by the Internet Service Provider (ISP).
(b) Search engine is a software used to search information on the internet.
(c) The World Wide Web is a collection of related websites.
(d) All of the above

27. Match the following lists.

| List I | List II |
|---|---|
| A.  | 1. Internet Explorer |
| B.  | 2. Opera |
| C.  | 3. Google Chrome |
| D.  | 4. Mozilla |

**Codes**

| | A | B | C | D | | A | B | C | D |
|---|---|---|---|---|---|---|---|---|---|
| (a) | 4 | 2 | 3 | 1 | (b) | 1 | 3 | 2 | 4 |
| (c) | 3 | 1 | 4 | 2 | (d) | 2 | 4 | 1 | 3 |

28. Match the following lists.

| | List I | List II |
|---|---|---|
| A. | WWW | 1. These pages form the building blocks of a website. |
| B. | Web browser | 2. The address or location of a web page |
| C. | Web page | 3. An application software that displays the webpage. |
| D. | URL | 4. A subset of internet |

**Codes**

| | A | B | C | D | | A | B | C | D |
|---|---|---|---|---|---|---|---|---|---|
| (a) | 1 | 2 | 4 | 3 | (b) | 4 | 3 | 1 | 2 |
| (c) | 2 | 4 | 3 | 1 | (d) | 3 | 1 | 2 | 4 |

29. Which of the following statements is correct about social networking site?
(a) It is a group of individuals who share their ideas, activities, messages, photos, videos etc.
(b) Some of the popular networking sites are Bing, Navigator, etc.
(c) It's not mandatory for a user to have a profile in a social networking site.
(d) It's not possible to upload a picture on a social networking site.

30. Which of the following statements is incorrect about web page?
(a) It contains the information in the form of text, graphics or sounds on the internet.
(b) A web page can be accessed through a web browser on the internet.
(c) There are three types of web pages - static, virtual and dynamic.
(d) Web pages form the building blocks of a website.

Darken your choice with HB Pencil

| | | | | | | | | | | | |
|---|---|---|---|---|---|---|---|---|---|---|---|
| 1. | (a) (b) (c) (d) | 6. | (a) (b) (c) (d) | 11. | (a) (b) (c) (d) | 16. | (a) (b) (c) (d) | 21. | (a) (b) (c) (d) | 26. | (a) (b) (c) (d) |
| 2. | (a) (b) (c) (d) | 7. | (a) (b) (c) (d) | 12. | (a) (b) (c) (d) | 17. | (a) (b) (c) (d) | 22. | (a) (b) (c) (d) | 27. | (a) (b) (c) (d) |
| 3. | (a) (b) (c) (d) | 8. | (a) (b) (c) (d) | 13. | (a) (b) (c) (d) | 18. | (a) (b) (c) (d) | 23. | (a) (b) (c) (d) | 28. | (a) (b) (c) (d) |
| 4. | (a) (b) (c) (d) | 9. | (a) (b) (c) (d) | 14. | (a) (b) (c) (d) | 19. | (a) (b) (c) (d) | 24. | (a) (b) (c) (d) | 29. | (a) (b) (c) (d) |
| 5. | (a) (b) (c) (d) | 10. | (a) (b) (c) (d) | 15. | (a) (b) (c) (d) | 20. | (a) (b) (c) (d) | 25. | (a) (b) (c) (d) | 30. | (a) (b) (c) (d) |

# 07

# Latest Developments in the Field of IT

1. What is the latest version of Windows Operating System?

(a) Windows 8.1 (b) Windows 10
(c) Windows 10.2 (d) Windows 8

2. …………… sensors are used in Internet of Things (IoT) systems and devices that are driven by pressure signals.

(a) Gas (b) Pressure
(c) Image (d) Temperature

3. Which company has launched 'Echo', an Artificial Intelligence enabled product ?

(a) Google (b) Philips (c) Amazon (d) Sony

4. What is Artificial Intelligence?

(a) Putting your intelligence into the computer
(b) Programming with your own intelligence
(c) Making a machine intelligent
(d) Making human being intelligent

5. What is Amazon?

(a) It is an American electronic commerce and cloud computing.
(b) It was founded by Jeff Bezos on 5th July, 1994.
(c) Amazon has separate retail websites for different companies.
(d) All of the above

6. Find the odd one out.

(a) Alexa (b) Cortana (c) Apple's Siri (d) Browser

7. Identify the name of the famous video game from the given image.

(a) Temple Run 6 (b) Bad Piggies
(c) Robolox (d) Tetris Attack

8. Internet provides us with an amazing facility of searching any .................. from any corner of the world.

(a) book (b) copy
(c) letter (d) information

9. Which is the best search engine in the world?

(a) Google (b) Yahoo
(c) Facebook (d) Binge

10. Which is the frame through which we see the website contents?

(a) New tab (b) Display window
(c) Menu bar (d) None of these

11. ............... provides us the connectivity to internet on payment of nominal charges.

(a) URL (b) LAN
(c) ISP (d) None of these

12. Which button lists the favourites?

(a) Home (b) Favourite
(c) Refresh (d) All of these

13. .............. allows the user to find previously viewed URLs.

(a) Home (b) Favourites
(c) Browser (d) History

14. What does 'tt' stand for in http?

(a) Transfer Text (b) Text Transfer
(c) Total Transfer (d) Transfer Total

15. Identify the given device in the picture.

(a) Amazon Echo
(b) Roomba
(c) Arlo Ultra
(d) Amazon Alexa

16. The given device in the picture is

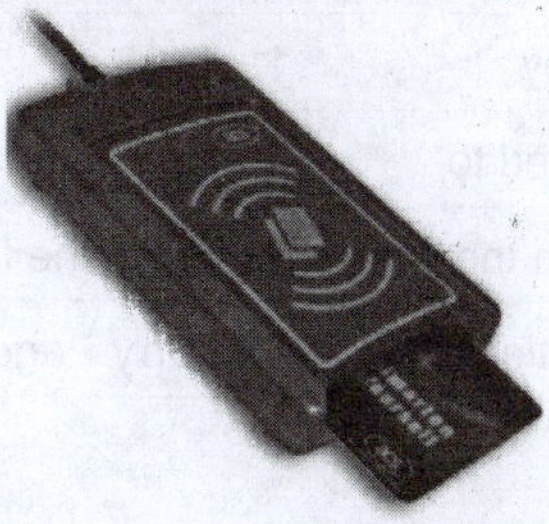

(a) Magnetic Ink Character Reader
(b) Smart Card Reader
(c) Magnetic Strip Reader
(d) OMR Reader

17. In the term BHIM, what does B stands for?
(a) Boost
(b) Best
(c) Bharat
(d) Beginner

18. When working on an Android app, the Android ………………….is required.
(a) Software Development Kit
(b) Software Delivery Kit
(c) Software Restoration Kit
(d) Software Integration Kit

19. Which of the following can capture moving video sequences as well as still images?
(a) Flatbed scanner
(b) Hand-held scanner
(c) Video digitizer
(d) Graphics tablet

20. Which of the following is/are true about Google Maps?
(a) It is a web mapping service available free of cost.
(b) It provides various geographical information and displays real-time traffic conditions.
(c) It directs the users to their destination and also shows the different modes of transport that can be used.
(d) All of the above

21. Which of the following statement(s) is/are false about desktop applications?

(a) There is no need to install desktop applications on the computer.

(b) These apps are represented as icons on the computer screen or as options in the Start menu.

(c) These apps can function without internet.

(d) All of the above

22. Match the following lists.

| | List I | List II |
|---|---|---|
| A. | Google was founded by | 1. 1996 |
| B. | Cloud computing is used to | 2. Upload file or folder |
| C. | Google was founded in the year | 3. Store the files and folder over internet |
| D. | Google Drive gives option to | 4. Larry Page and Sergey Brin |

**Codes**

| | A | B | C | D | | A | B | C | D |
|---|---|---|---|---|---|---|---|---|---|
| (a) | 3 | 4 | 1 | 2 | (b) | 4 | 3 | 1 | 2 |
| (c) | 4 | 1 | 2 | 3 | (d) | 3 | 2 | 1 | 4 |

Darken your choice with HB Pencil

| | | | | | | | | | | | |
|---|---|---|---|---|---|---|---|---|---|---|---|
| 1. | ⓐ ⓑ ⓒ ⓓ | 5. | ⓐ ⓑ ⓒ ⓓ | 9. | ⓐ ⓑ ⓒ ⓓ | 13. | ⓐ ⓑ ⓒ ⓓ | 17. | ⓐ ⓑ ⓒ ⓓ | 21. | ⓐ ⓑ ⓒ ⓓ |
| 2. | ⓐ ⓑ ⓒ ⓓ | 6. | ⓐ ⓑ ⓒ ⓓ | 10. | ⓐ ⓑ ⓒ ⓓ | 14. | ⓐ ⓑ ⓒ ⓓ | 18. | ⓐ ⓑ ⓒ ⓓ | 22. | ⓐ ⓑ ⓒ ⓓ |
| 3. | ⓐ ⓑ ⓒ ⓓ | 7. | ⓐ ⓑ ⓒ ⓓ | 11. | ⓐ ⓑ ⓒ ⓓ | 15. | ⓐ ⓑ ⓒ ⓓ | 19. | ⓐ ⓑ ⓒ ⓓ | | |
| 4. | ⓐ ⓑ ⓒ ⓓ | 8. | ⓐ ⓑ ⓒ ⓓ | 12. | ⓐ ⓑ ⓒ ⓓ | 16. | ⓐ ⓑ ⓒ ⓓ | 20. | ⓐ ⓑ ⓒ ⓓ | | |

# Practice Sets

## 1-3

# Practice Set 01

Time : 60 Mins. Max. Marks : 35

**General Instructions**

1. This question paper contains 35 questions.
2. All questions are compulsory. There is no negative marking.
3. Use HB pencil / Blue ball point pen to mark your choice of answer by darkening the circles on the OMR Sheet.

1. Monitor, printer, plotter and speakers are
(a) Output device (b) Hardware device
(c) Input device (d) None of these

2. Which shortcut key is used to select the whole drawing?
(a) CTRL + A (b) CTRL + B
(c) CTRL + C (d) CTRL + D

3. What is World Wide Web?
(a) App
(b) Game
(c) Another name of internet
(d) A system of internet servers that support specially formatted documents.

4. Which of the following devices incorporates a small computing chip?
(a) Smartphone (b) Car security system
(c) Smart watch (d) All of these

5. CD stands for
(a) Common Drive (b) Compact Disk
(c) Control Disk (d) Compact Drive

6. What is an example of an Operating System?
(a) Word (b) Excel (c) Windows 7 (d) Paint

7. The size of the area in which you want to type the text or align the text can be set by
(a) scroll bar (b) ruler
(c) status bar (d) None of these

**8.** An android mobile Operating System was developed by

(a) Microsoft (b) Apple Inc.

(c) Google (d) IBM

**9.** ................. controls the movement of information between the memory, the ALU and other parts of computer.

(a) Logical Unit (b) Control Unit

(c) Secondary Unit (d) Primary Unit

**10.** .................. option is used to customise the wallpaper.

(a) Quick Launch bar (b) Personalize

(c) View (d) Date and Time settings

**11.** Cutting and pasting a sentence is known as

(a) text editing (b) text formatting

(c) indentation (d) text wrapping

**12.** Google Hangouts is a

(a) group (b) document

(c) free video chat service (d) Search engine

**13.** The site Wikipedia.org provides an

(a) online encyclopedia (b) online news

(c) online dictionary (d) online game

**14.** .................... is the shortcut key to open a new file in MS Paint.

(a) File + Open (b) CTRL + N

(c) Open (d) CTRL + X

**15.** Computer needs ................. to perform any work.

(a) pen drive (b) hardware

(c) software (d) Both (b) and (c)

**16.** Which of the following devices is used to store information permanently?

(a)  (b) 

(c)  (d) 

17. What is the name of this tool?

(a) Eraser (b) Pencil
(c) Fill with color (d) Magnifier

18. Identify the image and choose the correct option.

(a) It creates a duplicate part of the selected text.
(b) It works with cut and copy options and places the text at the required place.
(c) It removes a selected text from a particular position and places it on the clipboard.
(d) All of the above

19. Identify the given app.

(a) Google Maps (b) Virtual Space App
(c) Google Play (d) None of these

20. Which of the following jumbled words is related to internet?
(a) SROWBER (b) TEKWORN
(c) GEPWABE (d) All of these

21. Select the correct process to hide the icons of the desktop screen.
(a) Right click → View → Uncheck show desktop icon
(b) Right click → View → Check show desktop icon
(c) Left click → View → Check show desktop icon
(d) Left click → View → Uncheck show desktop icon

22. Select the incorrect statement.
(a) Light pen and Joystick are pointing devices.
(b) OMR is a special type of scanner used to evaluate MCQ answer sheets.
(c) Webcam is used to give sound output.
(d) Plotter is used for designing purposes.

23. .............. is a permanent memory in computers.
(a) ROM
(b) Auxiliary memory
(c) Blu - ray disc
(d) None of these

24. All files deleted from the computer are stored in ................. of Windows 7.
(a) Recent Place
(b) Recycle Bin
(c) My Document
(d) Network Place

25. Which is not a type of scroll bar?
(a) Vertical scroll bar
(b) Straight bar
(c) Horizontal scroll bar
(d) All of these

26. .................... command is not present in the Quick Access Toolbar.
(a) Draw Table
(b) E-mail
(c) Print Preview
(d) Prepare

27. Sending the file over the internet is known as
(a) uploading
(b) downloading
(c) accessing
(d) logging

28. Select the incorrect match.
(a) Shopping site
(b) Social Networking Service
(c) Search Engine
(d) Messaging App

29. Which of the following is/are automatically counted in MS Word?
(a) Number of words
(b) Number of pages
(c) Number of characters
(d) All of these

30. The zoom option is present in which tab?
(a) Edit tab
(b) File tab
(c) Image tab
(d) View tab

31. The File Explorer options dialog box comes with how many tabs?
(a) Two
(b) Three
(c) Four
(d) Five

32. Full stop, dot, comma are associated with which key?

(a) Backspace key (b) Punctuation key

(c) Arrow key (d) Shift key

33. Match the following lists.

| | List I | | List II |
|---|---|---|---|
| A. | Abacus | 1. | Commonly operated machines used In technical and educational research |
| B. | Computer | 2. | First mechanical calculating device |
| C. | Computer system | 3. | A memory unit used by first generation of computer |
| D. | Counter wheels | 4. | Hardware, software and peripheral devices |

**Codes**

| | A | B | C | D | | A | B | C | D |
|---|---|---|---|---|---|---|---|---|---|
| (a) | 3 | 1 | 4 | 2 | (b) | 2 | 4 | 3 | 1 |
| (c) | 3 | 4 | 1 | 2 | (d) | 2 | 1 | 4 | 3 |

34. A program that searches for web documents with keyboards you specify

(a) search engine (b) E-mail

(c) website (d) folder

35. If you make a mistake when creating or editing a word document you can roll back to your previous work by using

(a) 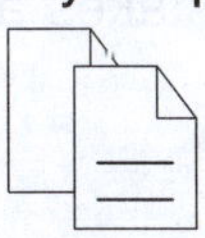

(b) 

(c) 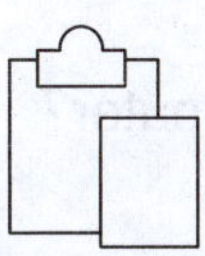

(d) 

Darken your choice with HB Pencil

| | | | | | | | | | | | |
|---|---|---|---|---|---|---|---|---|---|---|---|
| 1. | a b c d | 7. | a b c d | 13. | a b c d | 19. | a b c d | 25. | a b c d | 31. | a b c d |
| 2. | a b c d | 8. | a b c d | 14. | a b c d | 20. | a b c d | 26. | a b c d | 32. | a b c d |
| 3. | a b c d | 9. | a b c d | 15. | a b c d | 21. | a b c d | 27. | a b c d | 33. | a b c d |
| 4. | a b c d | 10. | a b c d | 16. | a b c d | 22. | a b c d | 28. | a b c d | 34. | a b c d |
| 5. | a b c d | 11. | a b c d | 17. | a b c d | 23. | a b c d | 29. | a b c d | 35. | a b c d |
| 6. | a b c d | 12. | a b c d | 18. | a b c d | 24. | a b c d | 30. | a b c d | | |

# Practice Set 02

Time : 60 Mins. Max. Marks : 35

**General Instructions**

1. This question paper contains 35 questions.
2. All questions are compulsory. There is no negative marking.
3. Use HB pencil / Blue ball point pen to mark your choice of answer by darkening the circles on the OMR Sheet.

**1.** Application that helps to download games on internet.

(a) flipkart.com

(b)

(c)

(d)

**2.** What color wavy line occurs under the text of any grammar mistakes and spelling mistakes in the document of MS Word 2016?

(a) Orange, Green (b) Green, Red
(c) Red, Black (d) Orange, Black

**3.** Which shortcut key is used to open the Start menu on the computer?

(a) Windows button (b) CTRL button
(c) F4 (d) CTRL + Shift

**4.** A computer cannot take its own decisions and it works only on man's orders, which means?

(a) It has no memory. (b) It is not accurate.
(c) It is versatile. (d) It has no IQ.

**5.** The hardware inside a computer includes

(a) Motherboard, CPU, RAM, hard drive
(b) Monitor, keyboard, mouse, speakers
(c) Cloud
(d) All of the above

6. It is used for zooming in and out of the drawing area.

(a) Select tool (b) Status bar
(c) Magnifier tool (d) Polygon tool

7. .................... is not a web browser.

(a) Mozilla (b) Internet Explorer
(c) Windows Explorer (d) Chrome

8. The first calculating machine which had wheels and gears was

(a) Pascaline (b) Calculator
(c) Punch Card (d) Difference Engine

9. After starting the window, a screen appears embedded with lots of icons. By which name is this screen popularly known as?

(a) Programs (b) Recycle Bin
(c) Desktop (d) My Documents

10. Microsoft Word is a

(a) computer hardware program
(b) computor non - application Program
(c) computer application program
(d) None of the above

11. An artificial environment having real life experiences like walking in space, without actually being in space is called

(a) virtual reality (b) multimedia
(c) graphics (d) animation

12. Identify the image and choose the correct option.

paytm

(a) It is the largest internet retailer in the world.
(b) It is owned by Facebook.
(c) It is an online service to play games.
(d) It is an Indian e-commerce payment system and digital wallet company.

13. .................. is a moving picture that appears when the computer is not used for some time.

(a) Icons (b) Screensaver
(c) Wallpaper (d) Clock

14. Which is common between a keyboard, mobile, casio and calculator?

(a) Style (b) Keys
(c) Size (d) All of these

15. Select the incorrect match.

(a) Pencil Tool 
(b) Line Tool 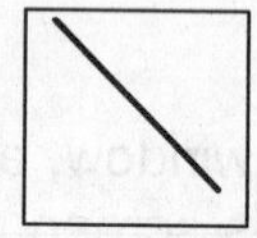
(c) Ellipse Tool 
(d) Eraser Tool 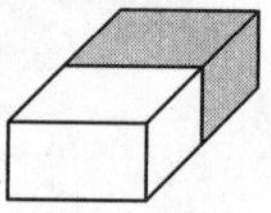

16. ...................... option will help you to send a birthday card to your friend with the help of a computer.

(a) E-Ticket (b) E-Book
(c) E-Mail (d) E-Learning

17. Which of the following languages does the computer understand?

(a) C Language (b) Assembly Language
(c) Basic Language (d) Binary Language

18. .................. feature of Windows 7 allows you to manage the functionality of keyboard and mouse.

(a) Control Panel (b) Status bar
(c) Windows Explorer (d) Internet Explorer

19. Select the odd one out.

(a) (b)
(c) (d)

20. E-mail address is made up of

(a) single part (b) two parts
(c) three parts (d) four parts

21. Drag and Drop is a technique to
(a) delete text (b) move text
(c) reformat text (d) All of these

22. To increase the thickness of the tool we press
(a) CTRL + + (b) CTRL + -
(c) CTRL + O (d) None of these

23. The concept of GUI come from
(a) Windows Operating System (b) My Computers
(c) My Documents (d) Desktop

24. Alphabet keys are .................... in number.
(a) 24 (b) 25
(c) 26 (d) 27

25. .................. use positional notation to represent a decimal number.
(a) Pascaline (b) Abacus
(c) Computer (d) Calculator

26. Identify the digital device

(a) 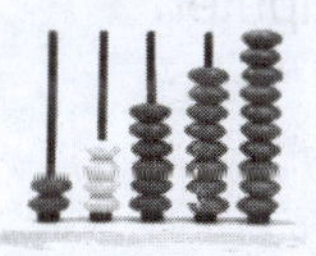 (b) 

(c)  (d) 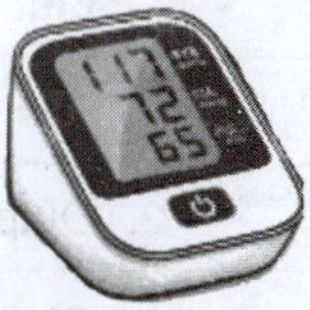



27. Identify the given app.

(a) It provides street location. (b) It is an activity tracker.
(c) It is a Glimpse. (d) All of these

28. Nowadays, everyone can watch Live Telecasts of Music Concerts, Award Functions, Cricket Matches, Republic Day Parade or Independence Day Flag hoisting on TV. TV channels use it to transmit their programs with the help of computers. What is it?
(a) Satellite (b) Rockets
(c) Space (d) Wires

29. Software which allows user to view the web page is called as
(a) Operating System (b) internet browser
(c) interpreter (d) Website

30. In color palette, we choose
(a) shapes (b) drawing
(c) color (d) strokes

31. What keyboard shortcut is applied to use the cut option?
(a) CTRL + C (b) CTRL + X
(c) CTRL + J (d) CTRL + V

32. In a computer, the user feeds the data using input devices, which is then passed to the CPU for processing and the result is stored and is displayed through the output devices. It acts as a central nervous system for a computer.
(a) Control Unit (b) Keyboard
(c) Flash drive (d) Mouse

33. Match the following lists.

| List I | List II |
|---|---|
| A. Hard copy | 1. The result displayed on monitor screen |
| B. Light pen | 2. Output that is printed on paper |
| C. Soft copy | 3. Computer understands instructions |
| D. Electrical signals | 4. Allows to draw on the screen |

**Codes**

| | A | B | C | D |
|---|---|---|---|---|
| (a) | 3 | 1 | 2 | 4 |
| (b) | 2 | 4 | 1 | 3 |
| (c) | 2 | 3 | 4 | 1 |
| (d) | 4 | 3 | 2 | 1 |

34. If we perform the following steps in MS Word 2016, then what will be the result?

 I. Typed MS Word 2016

 II. Pressed Backspace key

 III. Pressed Delete key

**Codes**

(a) MS Word 2016 (b) MS Word 201

(c) MS Word 16 (d) MS Word 21

35. Choose the correct option on the basis of the statements given regarding Windows 7.

 I. You can use this option when you are going to be away from your computer for just a little while or 5 minutes break.

 II. It makes the computer go into low-power state.

 III. Within few seconds, you can again resume your work from where you left.

**Codes**

(a) Shutdown (b) Switch User

(c) Restart (d) Sleep

Darken your choice with HB Pencil

| | | | | | | | | | | | |
|---|---|---|---|---|---|---|---|---|---|---|---|
| **1.** | ⓐ ⓑ ⓒ ⓓ | **7.** | ⓐ ⓑ ⓒ ⓓ | **13.** | ⓐ ⓑ ⓒ ⓓ | **19.** | ⓐ ⓑ ⓒ ⓓ | **25.** | ⓐ ⓑ ⓒ ⓓ | **31.** | ⓐ ⓑ ⓒ ⓓ |
| **2.** | ⓐ ⓑ ⓒ ⓓ | **8.** | ⓐ ⓑ ⓒ ⓓ | **14.** | ⓐ ⓑ ⓒ ⓓ | **20.** | ⓐ ⓑ ⓒ ⓓ | **26.** | ⓐ ⓑ ⓒ ⓓ | **32.** | ⓐ ⓑ ⓒ ⓓ |
| **3.** | ⓐ ⓑ ⓒ ⓓ | **9.** | ⓐ ⓑ ⓒ ⓓ | **15.** | ⓐ ⓑ ⓒ ⓓ | **21.** | ⓐ ⓑ ⓒ ⓓ | **27.** | ⓐ ⓑ ⓒ ⓓ | **33.** | ⓐ ⓑ ⓒ ⓓ |
| **4.** | ⓐ ⓑ ⓒ ⓓ | **10.** | ⓐ ⓑ ⓒ ⓓ | **16.** | ⓐ ⓑ ⓒ ⓓ | **22.** | ⓐ ⓑ ⓒ ⓓ | **28.** | ⓐ ⓑ ⓒ ⓓ | **34.** | ⓐ ⓑ ⓒ ⓓ |
| **5.** | ⓐ ⓑ ⓒ ⓓ | **11.** | ⓐ ⓑ ⓒ ⓓ | **17.** | ⓐ ⓑ ⓒ ⓓ | **23.** | ⓐ ⓑ ⓒ ⓓ | **29.** | ⓐ ⓑ ⓒ ⓓ | **35.** | ⓐ ⓑ ⓒ ⓓ |
| **6.** | ⓐ ⓑ ⓒ ⓓ | **12.** | ⓐ ⓑ ⓒ ⓓ | **18.** | ⓐ ⓑ ⓒ ⓓ | **24.** | ⓐ ⓑ ⓒ ⓓ | **30.** | ⓐ ⓑ ⓒ ⓓ | | |

# Practice Set 03

Time : 60 Mins. Max. Marks : 35

**General Instructions**

1. This question paper contains 35 questions.
2. All questions are compulsory. There is no negative marking.
3. Use HB pencil / Blue ball point pen to mark your choice of answer by darkening the circles on the OMR Sheet.

**1.** RAM stands for

(a) Recent Actual Memory (b) Random Access Memory

(c) Recent Average Memory (d) Random Actual Memory

**2.** MS Paint can be achieved by using

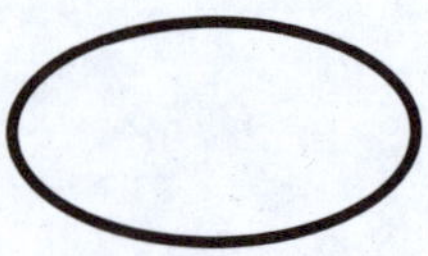

(a) Line tool (b) Oval tool

(c) Paint tool (d) None of these

**3.** Pick the odd one out.

(a)  (b) 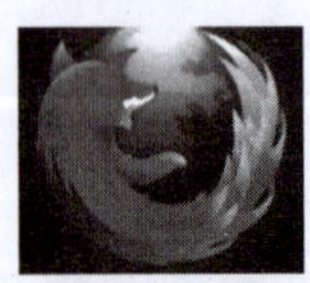

(c)  (d) 

**3.** Which of the following is incorrect about CPU?

(a) It is a processing device of a computer.

(b) It controls the input and output devices attached to a computer.

(c) It processes instructions, performs calculations and manages information through a computer system.

(d) It is also known as Visual Display Unit.

**4.** A......................is not a component of Desktop.

(a) icon (b) Taskbar

(c) minimise button (d) Start button

**5.** Which of the following is present in Alignment Option?

(a) Align text left (b) Center

(c) Align text right (d) All of these

**6.** Cloud is an online file storage service given by

(a) IBM (b) Microsoft

(c) Google (d) Apple

**7.** .................. key is used to type capital letters when the caps lock is off.

(a) Space bar (b) Caps lock

(c) Control (d) Shift

**8.** The blank area in the centre in MS-Paint is called

(a) the drawing area (b) blank area

(c) cool area (d) plane area

**9.** ISP is an acronym that refers to a company that provides

(a) free books (b) internet connection

(c) list of nearby shops (d) shelter to needy

**10.** These devices connect computer components so that they may communicate with each other. It can be more than one in a system.

(a) Cables (b) Diskettes

(c) Headphones (d) Keys

**11.** File Explorer in Windows 10 allows to

(a) visit folders (b) create folders

(c) Both (a) and (b) (d) None of these

**12.** Which option(s) is/are correct to save the document in MS Word?

(a) Save (b) Save As

(c) CTRL + S (d) All of these

**13.** Which of the following mouse pointer shape is displayed when used for website links?

(a)  (b)  (c)  (d) 

14. In MS Paint, which of these image properties can you change using the Image Properties Dialog Box?
(a) Units (b) Colors
(c) Dimensions (d) All of these

15. A person who designs the programs in a software package is called:
(a) user (b) software programmer
(c) system developer (d) system manager

16. Which of the following computer languages is written in binary codes only?
(a) Pascal (b) C
(c) Machine language (d) C#

17. Which one is the basic input device in GUI ?
(a) Voice System (b) Mouse
(c) Touch Panel (d) None of these

18. Which of the following is not a version of the Android Operation System?
(a) Red Hat (b) Nougat
(c) Lollipop (d) Marshmallow

19. ...................... is a collection of linked documents that contain text and other media elements such as graphics, animation, video or audio.
(a) Web server (b) URL
(c) Website (d) Search tools

20. By clicking on what we can get the picture back to normal size?
(a) Zoom to 25% (b) Zoom to 50%
(c) Zoom to 100% (d) Zoom to 200%

21. First Graphical User Interface (GUI) used commercially, was introduced in
(a) 1975 (b) 1970
(c) 1980 (d) 1983

22. Which of the following is not an example of system software?
(a) Word processors (b) Language translators
(c) Operating software (d) Utility software

23. ................. controls the functioning of all the parts of a computer.
(a) Control unit (b) Memory unit
(c) Input unit (d) Arithmetic Logical Unit

24. The output quality of a printer is measured by ................ inch.

(a) pixels per square
(b) dots per square
(c) cm per square
(d) numbers per square

25. In MS Paint, a picture can be skewed

(a) horizontally but not vertically
(b) vertically but not horizontally
(c) Both horizontally and vertically
(d) None of the above

26. Identify the given image.

(a) Joystick
(b) Selfie stick
(c) Pendrive
(d) Microphone

27. The given image shows the .................. of computer with ................ .

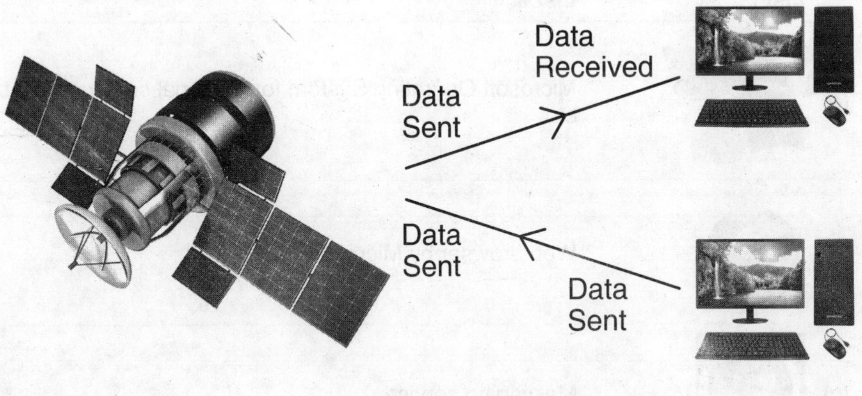


(a) disconnection, satellite
(b) connection, tablet
(c) connection, satellite
(d) disconnection, remote

28. With which of the following devices the symbol shown here relates?

(a)  (b)  (c)  (d) 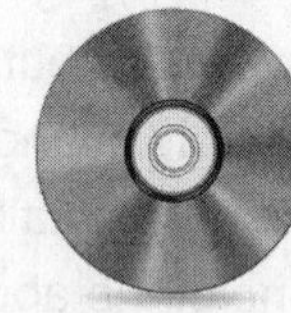

29. How can File Explorer options be changed in Windows 10?

(a) By using Control Panel
(b) By using File Explorer context menu
(c) By using Microsoft Edge settings
(d) None of these

30. In MS Paint, which tool is selected by default?

(a) Text
(b) Brushes
(c) Paint
(d) Eraser

31. What was the initial name of Microsoft Word, when it was released?

(a) Multi - Technique Word
(b) Multi - Transition Word
(c) Multi - Type Word
(d) Multi - Tool Word

32. Which of the following icon is incorrectly matched with its description?

| | List I | List II |
|---|---|---|
| (a) |  | Microsoft Operating System for personal computers, tablets etc. |
| (b) |  | Web browser by Microsoft |
| (c) |  | Messaging service |
| (d) |  | Popular gaming app |

**33.** Which of the following statement is correct for PlayStation 4?

(a) A keyboard specially designed for blind people.

(b) A home video game console.

(c) A social networking site only for video game players.

(d) An online service to play video games with your added friends.

**34.** Office button is symbolised with which feature on MS Word?

(a) Paper (b) Ribbon

(c) Arrow (d) Office

**35.** Choose the correct statement(s) for Windows taskbar.

(a) Identifies the path for the currently open folder.

(b) Software that controls the basic operations of the computer.

(c) Appears at the bottom of the screen and displays icons of programs that are easily accessible.

(d) All of the above

**Darken your choice with HB Pencil**

| | | | | | | | | | | | |
|---|---|---|---|---|---|---|---|---|---|---|---|
| **1.** | ⓐ ⓑ ⓒ ⓓ | **7.** | ⓐ ⓑ ⓒ ⓓ | **13.** | ⓐ ⓑ ⓒ ⓓ | **19.** | ⓐ ⓑ ⓒ ⓓ | **25.** | ⓐ ⓑ ⓒ ⓓ | **31.** | ⓐ ⓑ ⓒ ⓓ |
| **2.** | ⓐ ⓑ ⓒ ⓓ | **8.** | ⓐ ⓑ ⓒ ⓓ | **14.** | ⓐ ⓑ ⓒ ⓓ | **20.** | ⓐ ⓑ ⓒ ⓓ | **26.** | ⓐ ⓑ ⓒ ⓓ | **32.** | ⓐ ⓑ ⓒ ⓓ |
| **3.** | ⓐ ⓑ ⓒ ⓓ | **9.** | ⓐ ⓑ ⓒ ⓓ | **15.** | ⓐ ⓑ ⓒ ⓓ | **21.** | ⓐ ⓑ ⓒ ⓓ | **27.** | ⓐ ⓑ ⓒ ⓓ | **33.** | ⓐ ⓑ ⓒ ⓓ |
| **4.** | ⓐ ⓑ ⓒ ⓓ | **10.** | ⓐ ⓑ ⓒ ⓓ | **16.** | ⓐ ⓑ ⓒ ⓓ | **22.** | ⓐ ⓑ ⓒ ⓓ | **28.** | ⓐ ⓑ ⓒ ⓓ | **34.** | ⓐ ⓑ ⓒ ⓓ |
| **5.** | ⓐ ⓑ ⓒ ⓓ | **11.** | ⓐ ⓑ ⓒ ⓓ | **17.** | ⓐ ⓑ ⓒ ⓓ | **23.** | ⓐ ⓑ ⓒ ⓓ | **29.** | ⓐ ⓑ ⓒ ⓓ | **35.** | ⓐ ⓑ ⓒ ⓓ |
| **6.** | ⓐ ⓑ ⓒ ⓓ | **12.** | ⓐ ⓑ ⓒ ⓓ | **18.** | ⓐ ⓑ ⓒ ⓓ | **24.** | ⓐ ⓑ ⓒ ⓓ | **30.** | ⓐ ⓑ ⓒ ⓓ | | |

# Answers *and* Explanations

## Chapter 1

1. (d) The biggest advantage of a computer is that it is automatic in its operation as the user has to give only the instructions to the computer, but does not have to explain the complete process to do the work.
2. (b) Humans get tired after doing work. Computers do not get tired as it can work for long hours without taking any rest or break and this quality of computers is called diligence.
3. (a) Data is the raw facts and figures which corresponds as the input by the user.
4. (a) A desktop computer is a personal computer designed for regular use at a single location on or near a desk or table.
5. (a) Supercomputers are the most powerful computers in the world. They are large in size and have high processing speed.
6. (d) Both Laptop and Palmtop had a rechargeable battery inside them.
7. (c) Desktop had to be fixed in one place and cannot be carried away easily.
8. (d) Microcomputer is also known as PC (Personal Computer), Digital computer or Desktop computer. It is a general purpose computer also used by students in school.
9. (a) A computer works on an IPO cycle whereas CPU (Central Processing Unit) is the brain of the computer.
10. (a) A computer produces output through the output devices, after input is taken and processing is done.
11. (c) ALU stands for Arithmetic Logical Unit does all the arithmetic calculations like addition, multiplication, subtraction and division. It also performs logical operations in a computer.
12. (c) A single digit of a number is known as bit, short name for binary digit.
13. (b)
14. (a) The speed of the first generation computers was in milli-seconds, i.e., thousands of a second.
15. (d) Memory is used to store the input as well as the processing and output of a computer. A computer has a large memory.
16. (c) The full form of CPU is Central Processing Unit is the part of a computer system that is also known as the brain of the computer.
17. (a) A laptop works on a rechargeable battery. It does not require direct power.
18. (b)
19. (d) Scientists use computers for their scientific research as well as for launching rockets into space.
20. (d) A computer has no IQ of its own. It cannot take decisions of its own. IQ means Intelligence Quotient.
21. (b)

**22.** (d) The part labelled as S is called Monitor. It is a device that is used to show the output, i.e., the end results.

**23.** (d) The part P called as the Central Processing Unit (CPU) consists of the Memory Unit, Control Unit and Arithmetic Logical Unit.

They help the CPU in controlling the input and output devices attached to a computer.

**24.** (d) A keyboard is used to give input to a computer. It does not have any memory or storage in it.

**25.** (c) In airports, the computers are used to book the tickets of the passengers.

**26.** (d)

**27.** (d) Computers are operated by direct power source, not a rechargeable battery.

**28.** (c) In offices, computers are mainly used for typing or printing letters, storing and retrieving data.

**29.** (a) **30.** (a)

## Chapter 2

**1.** (b) **2.** (d) **3.** (a) **4.** (d)

**5.** (c) The image of the storage device is pen drive. It is very small, but it can store a huge amount of data. It can be used to transfer data from one computer to another. It is also known as a flash drive.

**6.** (a) **7.** (b)

**8.** (b) A Laptop is an all in one computing machine. It supports a touchpad which is used in place of a mouse to select and open items.

**9.** (a) The keyboard is the most commonly used input device. It is used to enter data and instructions into a computer. Monitor displays the output produced by the computer after processing the input.

**10.** (c) Input and Output devices are also known as Computer Peripherals, that connect the computer to different things to add functionality. Examples - mouse, keyboard, monitor etc.

**11.** (a) Continuous stationery paper is a long strip of paper, which is used for printing invoices. Dot matrix printers provide support for continuous stationery.

**12.** (c) The Hard disk is an in-built storage device in which data is stored by default. It looks like a small box, which is fixed inside the CPU cabinet.

**13.** (b) Spacebar key is the longest key on the keyboard. It is used to give space between two letters, words and numbers by pressing it.

**14.** (d) A keyboard is an input device with 104 keys. Each key denotes either an alphabet, number or number commands, which can be given to a computer for various actions to be performed. It is a modified version of typewriter keys.

**15.** (b) In order to print something, press Ctrl + P. There is no separate key to print. The Ctrl key and P alphabet key are pressed at the same time for the print command.

**16.** (a) Application Software is a group of programs designed for the end users. This software is created for a specific purpose and performs coordinated functions and tasks for the benefit of users.

**17.** (c) A monitor looks like a television. It displays the output produced after processing the input. It can show both text and pictures. That is why it is also known as the Visual Display Unit.

**18.** (b) The light pen is a wand - like looking input device, which can be directly moved over the device's screen and is light - sensitive.

**19.** (c) A scanner is an input device that reads the text or pictures printed on a sheet and transfers it to a computer. Eg. a printed or a handwritten document, photographs etc. A flatbed scanner is the most commonly used scanner.

**20.** (b) The Motherboard also known as Mainboard or System board, is the main circuit present inside the CPU cabinet. It holds together other parts of a computer including CPU, memory and connectors for input and output devices.

**21.** (c) The Enter key is used to move the cursor to the next new line. A keyboard usually has 2 Enter keys.

**22.** (a) Microsoft Word is an example of Application software. Application softwares are easier to design and are written in high level language. They are easier to use and manipulate.

**23.** (c) The mouse controls the movement of the cursor on the monitor. It has two buttons - left button and right button. It also has a scroll wheel in the middle of them.

**24.** (d) The images (a), (b) and (c) are : microphone, joystick and scanner, which are input devices whereas the image (d) is a printer, an output device.

**25.** (b)

**26.** (c) The backspace key is used to erase the letters or words to the left of the cursor.

**27.** (b) **28.** (b)

**29.** (a) F1, F2,....F12 are function keys. These keys act as shortcuts in performing certain functions like saving files, refreshing a page, etc.

**30.** (d) **31.** (b) **32.** (a)

## Chapter 3

**1.** (a) **2.** (c) **3.** (b) **4.** (b) **5.** (c) **6.** (b) **7.** (a)

**8.** (c) CUI stands for Character User Interface, where a user interacts with a computer using only a keyboard.

**9.** (c) **10.** (a) **11.** (c) **12.** (b) **13.** (a)

**14.** (b) The Start menu is a list of options that opens by clicking on the Start button. The start menu has two parts- left pane and right pane.

**15.** (a) **16.** (a)

**17.** (b) File Explorer is a file manager application of Windows.

**18.** (d) **19.** (b) **20.** (c) **21.** (d) **22.** (d) **23.** (c) **24.** (b) **25.** (b) **26.** (d) **27.** (b)

**28.** (a) **29.** (c) **30.** (d) **31.** (b) **32.** (c) **33.** (a)

## Chapter 4

**1.** (c) **2.** (b) **3.** (a) **4.** (a) **5.** (c) **6.** (d) **7.** (a)

**8.** (c) The paint window is divided into three distinct subsections : the Canvas, the Status Bar and the Menu Bar.

**9.** (a) The line tool allows to create straight lines that are perpendicular or tangent to objects.

**10.** (b) Magnifier Tool in paint is used to zoom in and zoom out the picture in the canvas area.

**11.** (b)

**12.** (c) In the Start Menu, click All Programs then Accessories and then click the Paint program.

**13.** (c) Clip Art is a type of graphic art. It is used extensively and comes in many forms, both electronic and printed.

**14.** (b)

**15.** (b) The 'airbrush' tool's button has the image of a paint can in it. The tool allows you to 'spray' an area of your image with the color of your choice.

**16.** (d) Default extension of paint file is .bmp.

.bmp full form bitmap image file is a raster graphics image file format used to store bitmap digital images, independently of the display device.

**17.** (a)

**18.** (a) To reverse the last action done by the user we can use the keyboard shortcut Ctrl+Z. We reverse more than one action using this shortcut tool.

**19.** (c) **20.** (d)

**21.** (b) The Quick Access Toolbar contains some commonly used predefined group of commands.

**22.** (d) **23.** (c) **24.** (d) **25.** (d)

**26.** (d) The image shown in option (d) is that of the Color Picker tool which is not a shape.

**27.** (d) **28.** (a) **29.** (d)

## Chapter 5

**1.** (b) Word processing refers to the act of using a computer to create, edit, save and print documents. Microsoft Word is an example of Word Processor.

**2.** (b) Magic tool is not available in MS Word but is available in Photoshop application. MS Word is a word processor application.

**3.** (a)

**4.** (b) We can save the document in MS Word in three ways-

(i) By clicking the file on the top left corner and then click Save As, where exactly you want to save the document on your computer.

(ii) By just pressing Ctrl+S.

(iii) By pressing F12.

**5.** (c) Superscript is a letter, character number or symbol that is set slightly for the normal line of type. It is generally smaller than the body of the text. Superscript is not related to the font style.

**6.** (c) **7.** (a) **8.** (b) **9.** (a) **10.** (d) **11.** (c) **12.** (a) **13.** (b) **14.** (a) **15.** (b)

**16.** (b) By selecting the Ruler option we can choose any of the Alignment types- Left Tab, Center Tab, Right Tab, Decimal Tab, Bar Tab and Horizontal Ruler.

**17.** (a) Redo is an option used to repeat the last work done in a document file. This option is available in the Quick Access Toolbar. The Redo button only appears after you have undone an action.

**18.** (d)

**19.** (a) Alt+F4 is a keyboard shortcut that completely closes the application you are currently using on your computer.

**20.** (a) Ctrl+S is the keyboard shortcut to save a document or file at any time. This option is available when the Auto-Save option is not selected.

**21.** (a) Exit is a command or option used to close a program or file. Click Exit on the File menu to close the document file.

**22.** (c) Click the File tab and select the Save As option. Select a folder where you would like to save the document, enter the file name which you want to give to your document and select the Save As option.

**23.** (c) In the given image, cut, copy and paste commands are shown. Using them, the tasks mentioned in options (a), (b) and (d) can be performed. But no command button is shown for the Redo operation, which is used for repeating the last operation done.

**24.** (a) Command button shown in option (a) is of Close file, which is present in File tab. The options (b), (c) and (d) are of Cut command, Paste command and Redo command.

**25.** (d) **26.** (c) **27.** (a) **28.** (b) **29.** (d)

## Chapter 6

**1.** (a) An Internet is a network of networks in which users at any one computer get information from any other computer (if they have permission) and sometimes may talk directly to users at other computers.

**2.** (d)

**3.** (a) The World Wide Web commonly referred to WWW refers to all the public websites or pages that users can access on their local computers and other devices through the internet.

**4.** (a) Tim Berners Lee invented the World Wide Web in 1989. He is a British computer scientist.

**5.** (c) Home page is the first page that is displayed after starting a Web Browser like Netscape's Navigator or Microsoft's Internet Explorer.

**6.** (b) The full form of virus is Vital Information Resource Under Siege. It is a program which interrupts the normal function of a computer system like memory, processing speed, data and programs.

**7.** (a) **8.** (d) **9.** (d) **10.** (c) **11.** (a) **12.** (b) **13.** (a) **14.** (d) **15.** (c) **16.** (a)

**17.** (b) **18.** (b) **19.** (a) **20.** (b) **21.** (d) **22.** (a) **23.** (c)

**24.** (d) A, B and C are the popular search engines, www.yahoo.com, www.google.com and www.bing.com. They are used to search information on the internet. Whereas option (d) is the image of Microsoft Internet Explorer, which is a web browser that enables the user to interact with text, images, videos, music and other information present on the internet.

**25.** (d) **26.** (d) **27.** (c) **28.** (b) **29.** (a) **30.** (c)

## Chapter 7

**1.** (b)

**2.** (b) Pressure sensors are used to detect and measure pressure.

**3.** (c) Amazon launched the product ECHO which are smart speakers.

**4.** (c) AI means making a machine intelligent.

**5.** (d)

**6.** (d) Except browser, other options are smart devices or features.

**7.** (c) **8.** (d) **9.** (a) **10.** (a) **11.** (c) **12.** (b) **13.** (d) **14.** (b) **15.** (a) **16.** (b)
**17.** (c) **18.** (a) **19.** (c) **20.** (d) **21.** (a) **22.** (b)

## Practice Set 1

| | | | | | | | | | | | | | | | | | | | |
|---|---|---|---|---|---|---|---|---|---|---|---|---|---|---|---|---|---|---|---|
| **1.** | (a) | **2.** | (a) | **3.** | (d) | **4.** | (d) | **5.** | (b) | **6.** | (c) | **7.** | (b) | **8.** | (c) | **9.** | (b) | **10.** | (b) |
| **11.** | (a) | **12.** | (c) | **13.** | (a) | **14.** | (b) | **15.** | (d) | **16.** | (c) | **17.** | (a) | **18.** | (c) | **19.** | (a) | **20.** | (d) |
| **21.** | (a) | **22.** | (c) | **23.** | (a) | **24.** | (b) | **25.** | (b) | **26.** | (d) | **27.** | (a) | **28.** | (c) | **29.** | (d) | **30.** | (d) |
| **31.** | (b) | **32.** | (b) | **33.** | (d) | **34.** | (a) | **35.** | (d) | | | | | | | | | | |

## Practice Set 2

| | | | | | | | | | | | | | | | | | | | |
|---|---|---|---|---|---|---|---|---|---|---|---|---|---|---|---|---|---|---|---|
| **1.** | (c) | **2.** | (b) | **3.** | (a) | **4.** | (d) | **5.** | (a) | **6.** | (c) | **7.** | (c) | **8.** | (a) | **9.** | (c) | **10.** | (c) |
| **11.** | (a) | **12.** | (d) | **13.** | (b) | **14.** | (b) | **15.** | (a) | **16.** | (c) | **17.** | (d) | **18.** | (a) | **19.** | (a) | **20.** | (c) |
| **21.** | (b) | **22.** | (a) | **23.** | (a) | **24.** | (c) | **25.** | (b) | **26.** | (d) | **27.** | (d) | **28.** | (a) | **29.** | (b) | **30.** | (c) |
| **31.** | (b) | **32.** | (a) | **33.** | (b) | **34.** | (b) | **35.** | (d) | | | | | | | | | | |

## Practice Set 3

| | | | | | | | | | | | | | | | | | | | |
|---|---|---|---|---|---|---|---|---|---|---|---|---|---|---|---|---|---|---|---|
| **1.** | (b) | **2.** | (b) | **3.** | (d) | **4.** | (c) | **5.** | (d) | **6.** | (d) | **7.** | (d) | **8.** | (a) | **9.** | (b) | **10.** | (a) |
| **11.** | (c) | **12.** | (d) | **13.** | (b) | **14.** | (d) | **15.** | (b) | **16.** | (c) | **17.** | (b) | **18.** | (a) | **19.** | (c) | **20.** | (c) |
| **21.** | (d) | **22.** | (a) | **23.** | (a) | **24.** | (b) | **25.** | (c) | **26.** | (b) | **27.** | (c) | **28.** | (b) | **29.** | (a) | **30.** | (b) |
| **31.** | (d) | **32.** | (d) | **33.** | (b) | **34.** | (b) | **35.** | (c) | | | | | | | | | | |